·VISUAL GUIDES·

SPORT MACHINES

·VISUAL GUIDES·

SPORT MACHINES

Norman Barrett

FRANKLIN WATTS

New York • Chicago • London • Toronto • Sydney

© 1994 Franklin Watts

Franklin Watts
95 Madison Avenue
New York, NY 10016

Library of Congress
Cataloging-in-Publication Data
Barrett, Norman S.
 Sport machines / Norman
Barrett.
 p. cm. – (Visual guides)
Includes index.
 ISBN 0-531-14299-X
 1. Motor vehicles –
Recreational use – Juvenile
literature.
 2. Recreation – Equipment
and supplies – Juvenile
literature.
 [1. Motor vehicles –
Recreational use.] I. Title.
II. Series: Barrett, Norman S.
Visual guides.
TL147.B2937 1994
796.5 – dc20   93-33236
               CIP   AC

A number of the illustrations in
this book appeared originally in
titles from the Picture Library,
Wheels and First Look series.

Series Editor
Norman Barrett

Designed by
K and Co

Picture Research by
Ruth Sonntag

Photographs by
Action Plus
Robert Bailey
N.S. Barrett
Bedford Trucks
Daytona International Speedway
Karting Magazine
Kawasaki Motors (UK) Ltd
Lewis Marine
Mistral
John Nicholson
Renault Cars Ltd
Ring Powercraft
Sadler International
Sward Sports
Thrust Cars Ltd
Timex

New Illustrations by
Rhoda and Robert Burns

Contents

Grand prix car

Grand prix is French for "big prize." Grand prix races are important events. The cars that take part in them have high-powered engines. Their drivers speed around the track for lap after lap. Some drop out or crash. The winner is the driver who finishes the required number of laps first.

▽ The grand prix car is a low-slung open-wheeler. It is built for speed – not only along the straights but also around the tight corners of the circuit.

Front wing

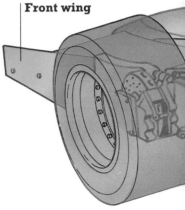

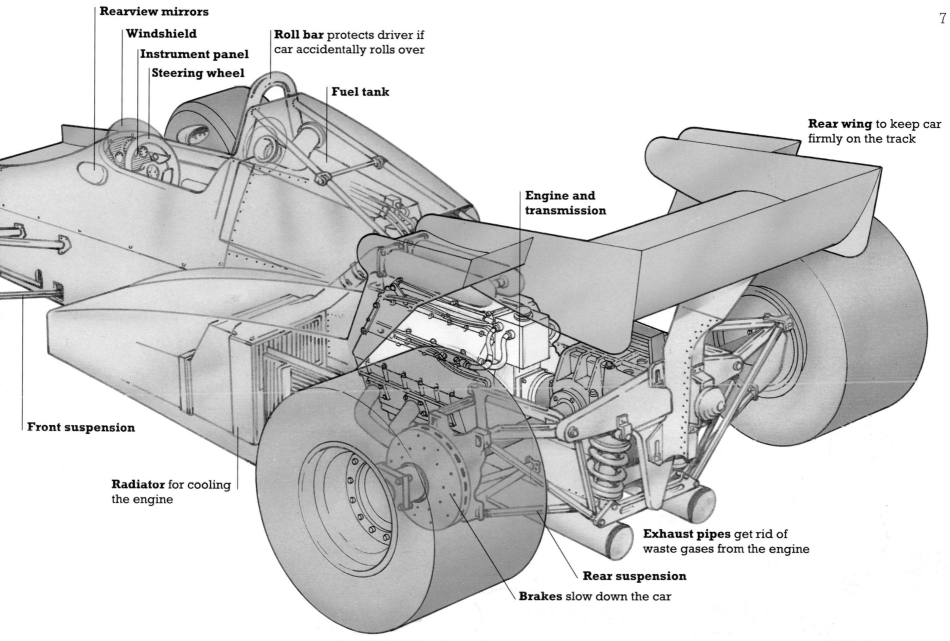

Rearview mirrors

Windshield

Instrument panel

Steering wheel

Roll bar protects driver if car accidentally rolls over

Fuel tank

Rear wing to keep car firmly on the track

Engine and transmission

Front suspension

Radiator for cooling the engine

Exhaust pipes get rid of waste gases from the engine

Rear suspension

Brakes slow down the car

Slicks – large smooth racing tires used for extra grip unless the track is wet

△ A top-fueler in
action. These dragsters
can reach speeds of
over 300 mph (485 km/h)
and cover the quarter-
mile track in less than
6 seconds.

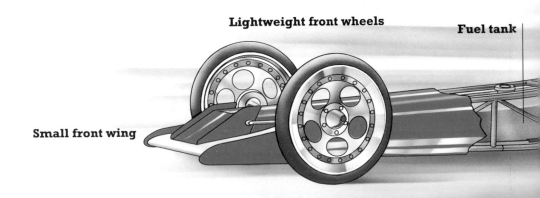

Lightweight front wheels

Fuel tank

Small front wing

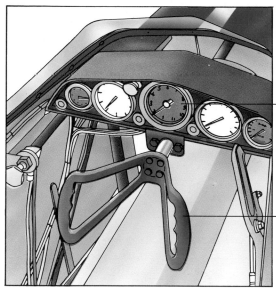

Instruments mounted in front of driver

Steering wheel

Dragster

Dragsters are the machines used in the sport of drag racing. They race in pairs on a special quarter-mile (402 m) track, or drag strip. A race lasts for no more than a few seconds, and the winner goes through to the next round.

The fastest dragsters are open-wheelers called "top fuelers."

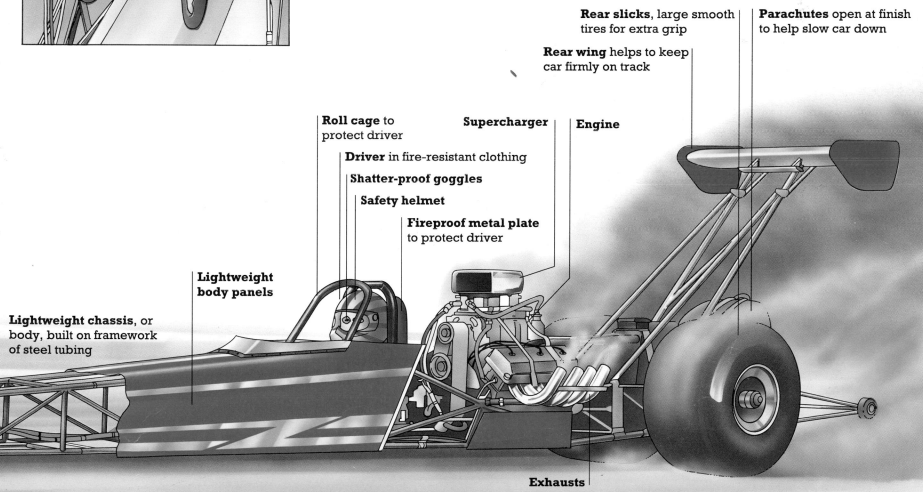

Rear slicks, large smooth tires for extra grip

Parachutes open at finish to help slow car down

Rear wing helps to keep car firmly on track

Roll cage to protect driver

Supercharger

Engine

Driver in fire-resistant clothing

Shatter-proof goggles

Safety helmet

Fireproof metal plate to protect driver

Lightweight body panels

Lightweight chassis, or body, built on framework of steel tubing

Exhausts

◁ Two karts battle for the lead as they take a sharp bend. In karting, the driver sits no more than 1 to 1½ inches (2 - 3 cm) from the ground.

Chain guard for protection in case transmission chain snaps

Kart

The kart is one of the simplest motorized racing machines. The sport of karting is like grand prix racing in miniature. There are classes for boys and girls as well as for adults.

Karts are powered by small engines. But the most powerful classes can reach speeds of 150 mph (240 km/h).

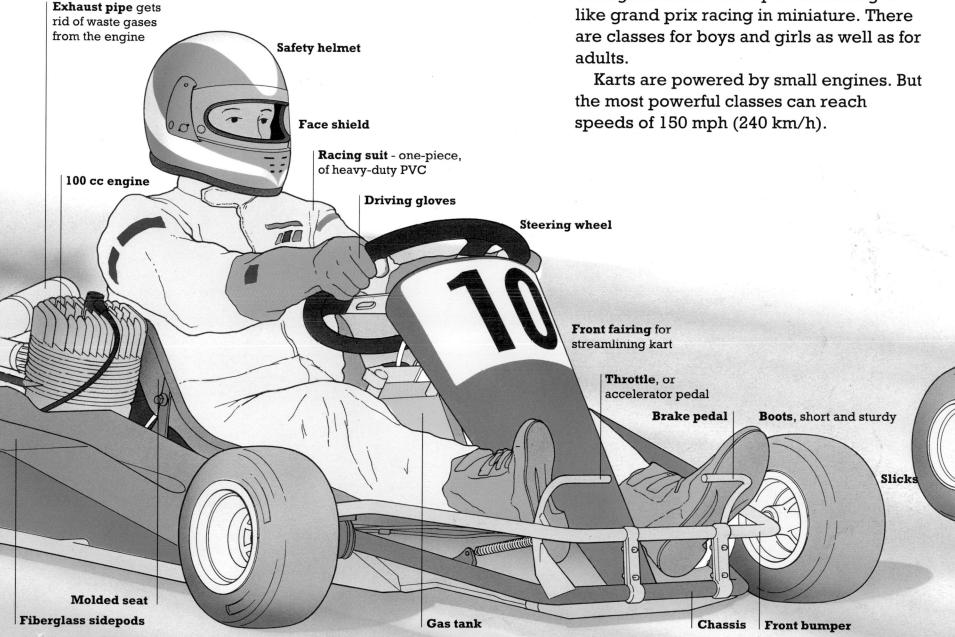

Exhaust pipe gets rid of waste gases from the engine

Safety helmet

Face shield

100 cc engine

Racing suit - one-piece, of heavy-duty PVC

Driving gloves

Steering wheel

Front fairing for streamlining kart

Throttle, or accelerator pedal

Brake pedal

Boots, short and sturdy

Slicks

Molded seat

Fiberglass sidepods

Gas tank

Chassis

Front bumper

◁ Stock cars take a turn at speed. The turns are banked (sloped up to the outside) to allow greater speeds when cornering. On a level track, a driver would have to take a turn much more slowly. Otherwise the car would tend to run straight off the track and into the wall.

Rear wing helps keep car on track at speed

Stock car

Stock car racing in the United States takes place on steeply banked oval tracks. The stock cars are based on current or recent hard-top models – like sedan car racing in Europe.

The engines of stock cars are designed to produce high speeds. But they run on regular gasoline.

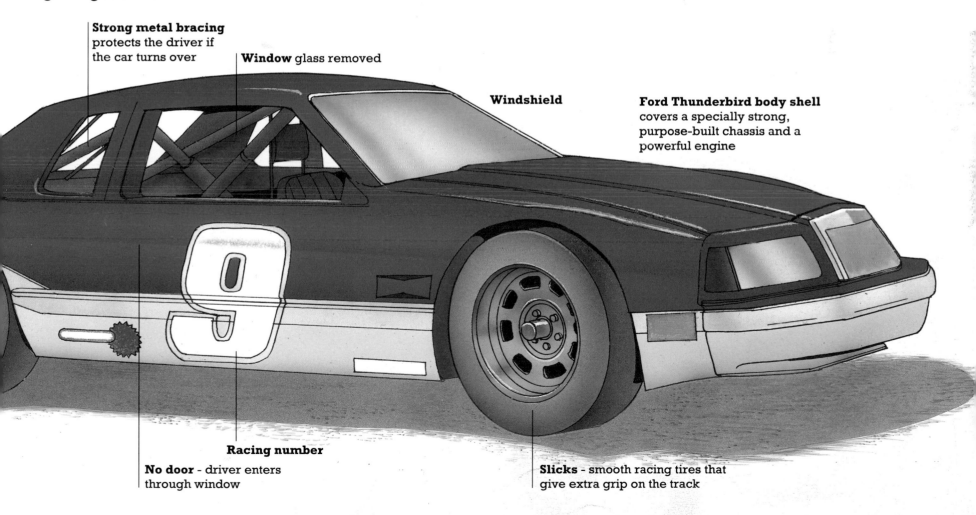

Strong metal bracing protects the driver if the car turns over

Window glass removed

Windshield

Ford Thunderbird body shell covers a specially strong, purpose-built chassis and a powerful engine

Racing number

No door - driver enters through window

Slicks - smooth racing tires that give extra grip on the track

◁ A rally car on a forest section of a rally. The driver is helped by a navigator, who reads the map. Rallies test cars and crews over different types of terrain, ranging from regular road surfaces to unpaved country ones.

Suspension strong enough to absorb buffeting from rough and bumpy ground

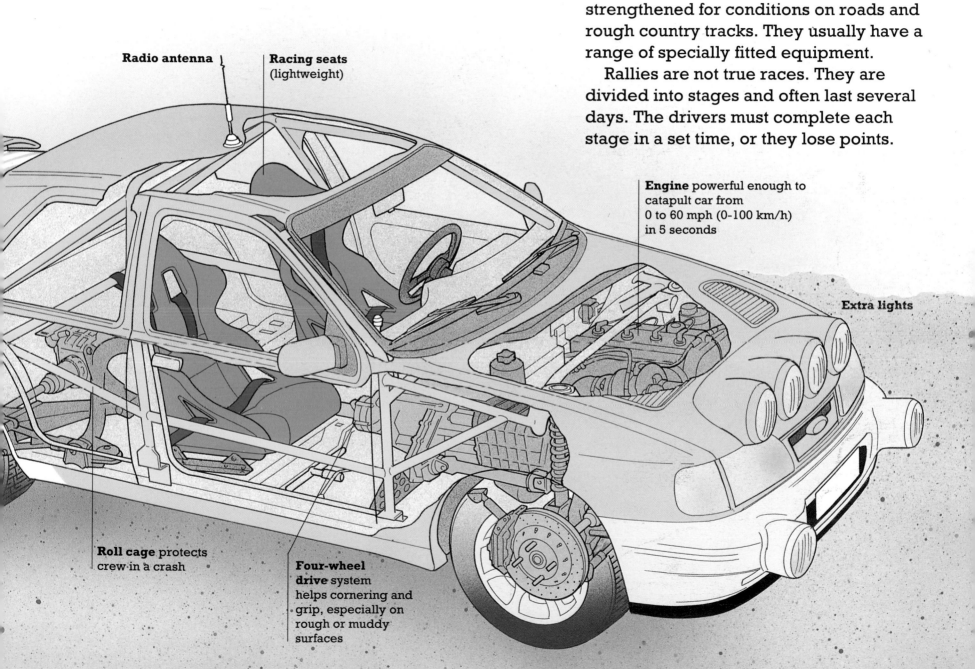

Rally car

Rally cars are ordinary sedan cars strengthened for conditions on roads and rough country tracks. They usually have a range of specially fitted equipment.

Rallies are not true races. They are divided into stages and often last several days. The drivers must complete each stage in a set time, or they lose points.

Radio antenna

Racing seats (lightweight)

Engine powerful enough to catapult car from 0 to 60 mph (0-100 km/h) in 5 seconds

Extra lights

Roll cage protects crew in a crash

Four-wheel drive system helps cornering and grip, especially on rough or muddy surfaces

Racing car progress

Grand prix racing cars have grown lighter and faster over the years. Improvements in materials and design have produced engines that are less than half the size of those that powered the cars in the early years of the sport. Yet modern racing cars lap the track at speeds more than double the highest speeds reached in those days.

△ **1912 Peugeot** (France)

△ **1924 Bugatti T35** (Germany/France)

◁ **1937 Mercedes-Benz W125** (Germany)

▽ **1948 Alfa Romeo 158** (Italy)

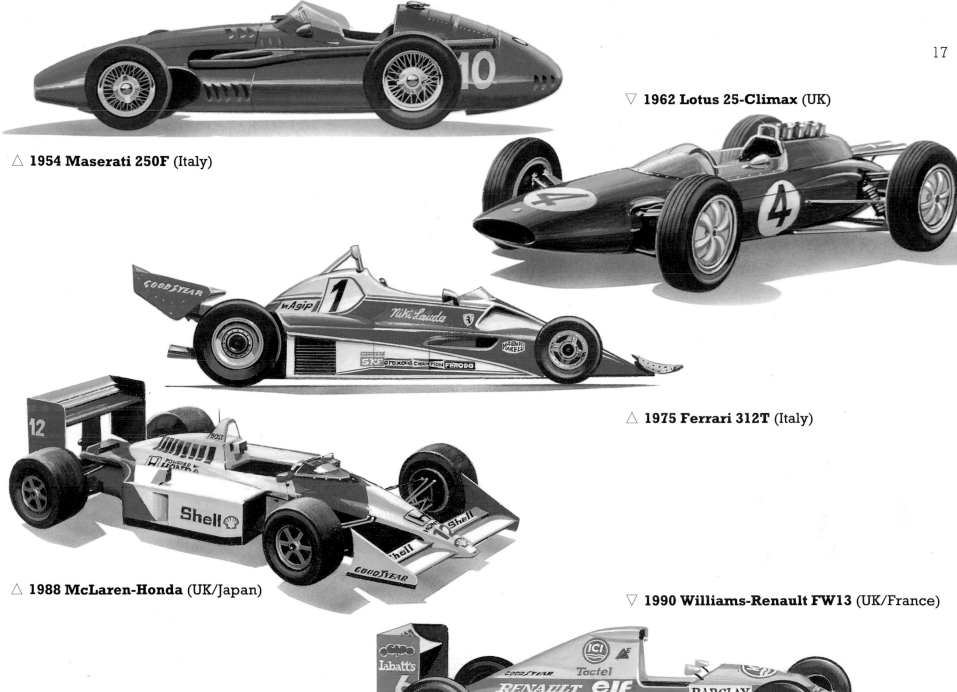

△ **1954 Maserati 250F** (Italy)

▽ **1962 Lotus 25-Climax** (UK)

△ **1975 Ferrari 312T** (Italy)

△ **1988 McLaren-Honda** (UK/Japan)

▽ **1990 Williams-Renault FW13** (UK/France)

Racing motorcycle

Motorcycle racing is the two-wheel version of motor racing. It also has grand prix events, with classes for various sizes of engine and for sidecars.

The sport is often known as road racing because it used to take place on highways. But grand prix races are now held on special circuits. A race consists of several laps of a circuit.

◁ Riders lean over at alarming angles as they take a corner at speed. They wear pads to protect their knees, which may scrape the ground when cornering. Racing motorcycles may look like road machines, but they are built for speed.

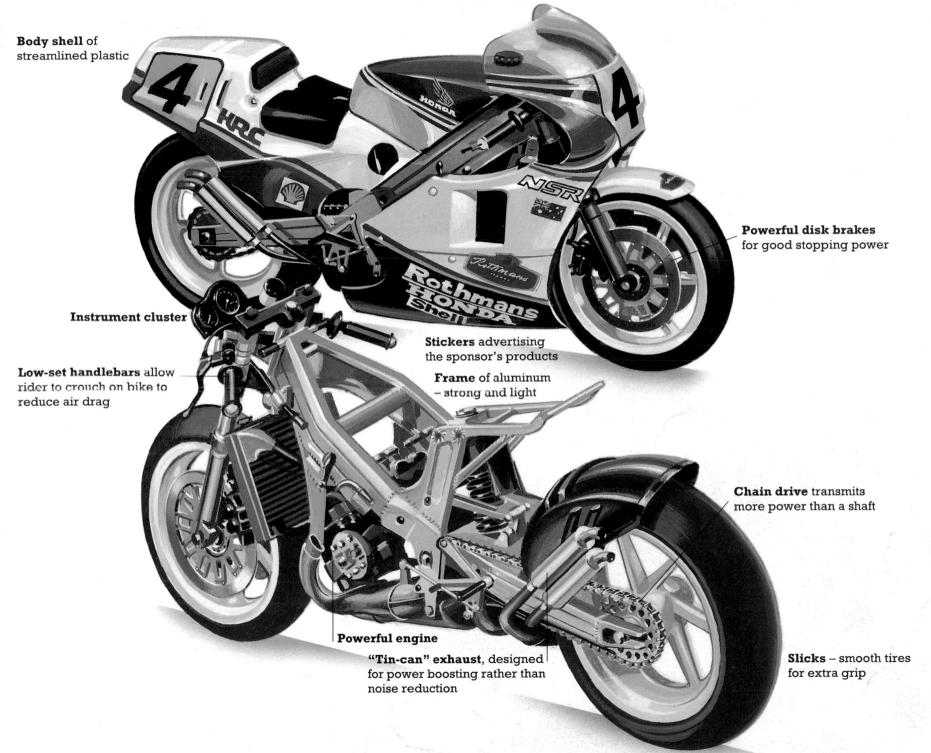

Body shell of streamlined plastic

Instrument cluster

Low-set handlebars allow rider to crouch on bike to reduce air drag

Powerful disk brakes for good stopping power

Stickers advertising the sponsor's products

Frame of aluminum – strong and light

Chain drive transmits more power than a shaft

Powerful engine

"Tin-can" exhaust, designed for power boosting rather than noise reduction

Slicks – smooth tires for extra grip

◁ Motocross takes place on specially marked courses in open country. The riders need excellent control to keep their machines upright on the rough ground.

Fender

Shock absorbers in front forks

Knobby tires for good grip on loose surfaces

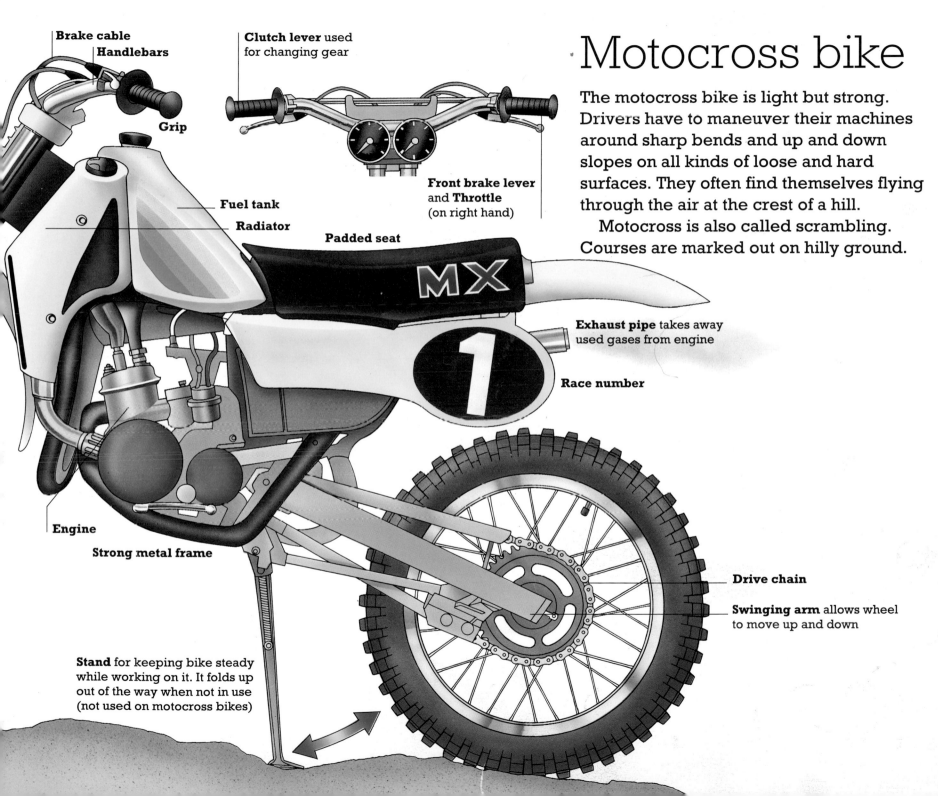

Brake cable

Handlebars

Grip

Clutch lever used for changing gear

Motocross bike

The motocross bike is light but strong. Drivers have to maneuver their machines around sharp bends and up and down slopes on all kinds of loose and hard surfaces. They often find themselves flying through the air at the crest of a hill.

Motocross is also called scrambling. Courses are marked out on hilly ground.

Front brake lever and **Throttle** (on right hand)

Fuel tank

Radiator

Padded seat

MX

Exhaust pipe takes away used gases from engine

1

Race number

Engine

Strong metal frame

Drive chain

Swinging arm allows wheel to move up and down

Stand for keeping bike steady while working on it. It folds up out of the way when not in use (not used on motocross bikes)

◁ Jumping through a hoop of fire is a thrilling stunt. But it can be dangerous if the proper precautions are not taken. The rider must wear special fire-resistant clothing and helpers must be at hand with fire extinguishers if needed.

2 Ramp set at precise angle for the jump. Bike leaves ramp at about 55-60 mph (90-95 km/h).

1 Bike accelerates toward take-off ramp.

3 Rider aims to keep bike upright with front wheel high in the air. Rear wheel keeps turning to prevent skidding when it hits landing ramp.

Stunt riding

Stunt riders use various kinds of machines, depending on the type of stunt they are performing.

Bikes used for the "big leap," as shown here, must be light and powerful. They must be able to reach a high speed to gain height and distance, and must have strong springs to absorb the shock on landing.

4 Bike drops toward ramp. With the correct take-off angle and speed, it should easily clear the last truck.

6 Bike and rider run off ramp and slow down.

5 Rear wheel of bike hits ramp first.

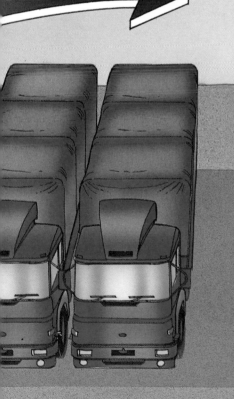

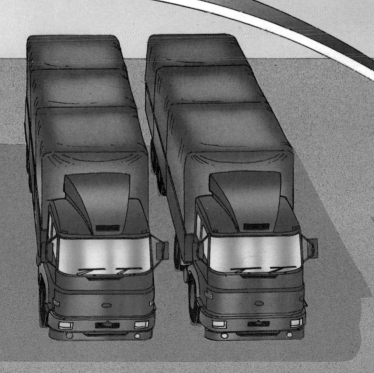

BMX bike

BMX bikes are tougher than most other bikes and have smaller tires. People ride them in races or other competitions.

Races are for up to eight riders. They race over a winding course laid out to include slopes, bumps, jumps, and sharp turns. In freestyle BMX, riders perform tricks and other routines.

◁ BMX tricks performed in midair are called "aerials." They are usually done by jumping off a steep ramp. Freestylers might have a landing drop of 10 feet (3 m) or more. Strong bikes are needed for this sort of rough treatment.

Padded cross-brace

Grips

Handlebars

Brake cable

Saddle

Adjustable seat clamp

Rear brake, compulsory in racing

Front brake, not essential in racing

Knobby tires for maximum grip on loose surfaces

Pedals, studded for extra grip

Frame

Cranks

Chainring

Forks

Alloy or steel rims

Racing yacht

People race in boats ranging from small one-person dinghies to large oceangoing yachts with a crew of ten or more.

Whatever the size of the boat, the basic principles of sailing are the same. The power of the wind, acting on the sail or sails, is used to move the boat through the water. It is steered by means of a rudder.

◁ This oceangoing Starlight-class yacht is used for racing and for leisure. It may be handled comfortably by two or three people. But for racing, when jobs such as hoisting sails must be done quickly, it could have a crew of eight or nine. The billowy colored sail is a spinnaker, used for making boats sail faster in light winds.

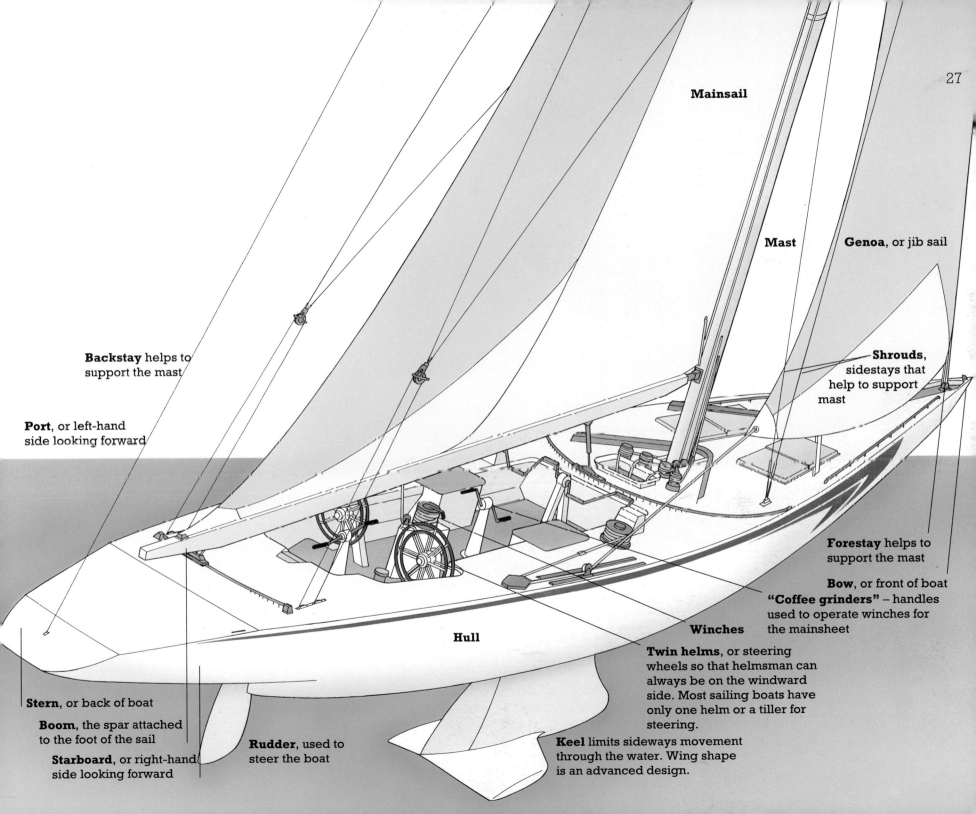

Mainsail

Mast

Genoa, or jib sail

Backstay helps to
support the mast

Shrouds,
sidestays that
help to support
mast

Port, or left-hand
side looking forward

Forestay helps to
support the mast

Bow, or front of boat

"Coffee grinders" – handles
used to operate winches for
the mainsheet

Winches

Hull

Twin helms, or steering
wheels so that helmsman can
always be on the windward
side. Most sailing boats have
only one helm or a tiller for
steering.

Stern, or back of boat

Boom, the spar attached
to the foot of the sail

Rudder, used to
steer the boat

Keel limits sideways movement
through the water. Wing shape
is an advanced design.

Starboard, or right-hand
side looking forward

◁ The windsurfer uses the boom for balance and for steering by controlling the position of the sail.

Uphaul rope, attached to boom, used for pulling rig up and out of water

Mast, made of fiberglass or aluminum, fits inside sleeve of the sail

Board, made of plastic or fiberglass

The sailboard is a simple craft, steered by means of the sail instead of a rudder. The sailor supports the mast and sail by holding the boom and using it to tilt the sail. The sport of boardsailing is also called windsurfing.

Window enables the windsurfer to see through the sail

Sail

Clew, eyelet for attaching boom to sail by outhaul rope

Boom, used for steering, changing speed, and keeping balance

Battens, to keep sail in shape, fit into pockets in sail

Daggerboard stops board slipping sideways through the water

Universal joint, connected to foot of mast, allows rig to swing completely around and to slant upward

Foot straps to help boardsailor keep feet in contact with the board when jumping

Skeg helps to keep board going in a straight line

Motorboat

Motorboats are streamlined racing machines that speed across lakes or through the waves of coastal waters. Classes of motorboats range from small one-seaters with outboard motors to cabin-class motorboats nearly 50 feet (15 m) long.

Many motorboats are equipped also for leisure activities. They have berths for sleeping, galleys for preparing food, and facilities for sunbathing and swimming.

▽ A motorboat speeds through the water with its bow (front) lifted up from the surface. This model, a Ring 26, does not look big, but it has a small cabin and galley below deck.

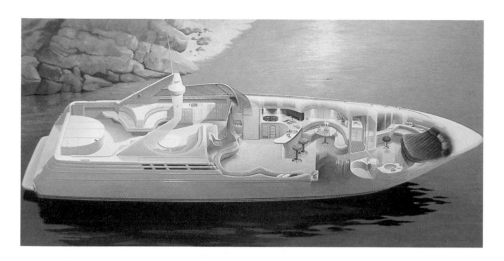

◁ A luxury motorboat, the Sea Ray Super 630 has a kitchen, bar, lounge, bathroom, and bedroom, as this below-deck cutaway shows. It is 63 feet (19.2 m) long, and although not a racing motorboat, can reach speeds of 44 knots (50 mph or 81 km/h).

▽ A cutaway of the Ring 26, a record breaker in its class with speeds of 60 knots (69 mph or 111 km/h).

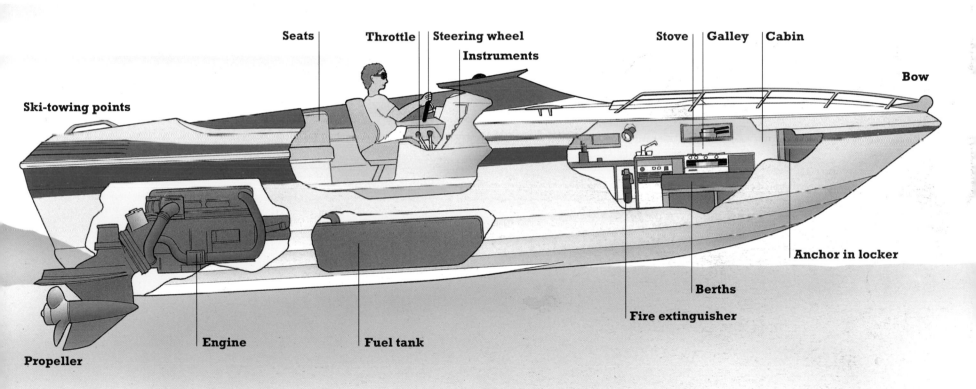

Seats **Throttle** **Steering wheel** **Stove** **Galley** **Cabin**

Instruments

Bow

Ski-towing points

Anchor in locker

Berths

Fire extinguisher

Engine **Fuel tank**

Propeller

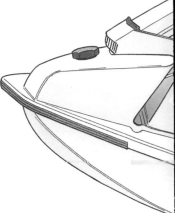

◁ Jet skiing is like
motorcycling on water.
To corner, the rider
turns the handlebars
and leans over. In the
event of a fall, the jet ski
rights itself and
automatically circles
back to the rider.

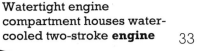

Watertight engine compartment houses water-cooled two-stroke **engine**

Water jet

Propeller turbine

Handlebars fold down for starting in a kneeling position

Starter and cut-out buttons on left-hand grip

Throttle on right-hand grip

Life preserver

△ The speed and direction of a jet ski are controlled by the force and angle of a jet of water. The engine drives an enclosed "impeller," or propeller turbine, which creates the jet.

Rubber-covered **non-slip platform**

Hull made of special fiberglass material for greater strength

Rear section filled with **waterproof foam** to make craft almost unsinkable

Jet ski

Jet skiing is one of the newest sports. People ride jet skis mainly for fun, but there is also jet ski racing. Speed and direction are controlled by a water jet.

As well as the solo jet ski, there are two-seater craft, with riders sitting either one behind the other or side by side. There is also a three-seater model.

Stern

Deck line provides a handhold

Deck

Hull, made of plastic or fiberglass

◁ A canoeist battles to keep his kayak balanced on a white-water course. White-water racing takes place on special river courses, with fast-flowing water and hazards such as weirs and rocks.

Leisure canoe has spade-type paddles, made of all wood or with a coated aluminum shaft and plastic or wooden blades

Helmets for use in rough and rocky water

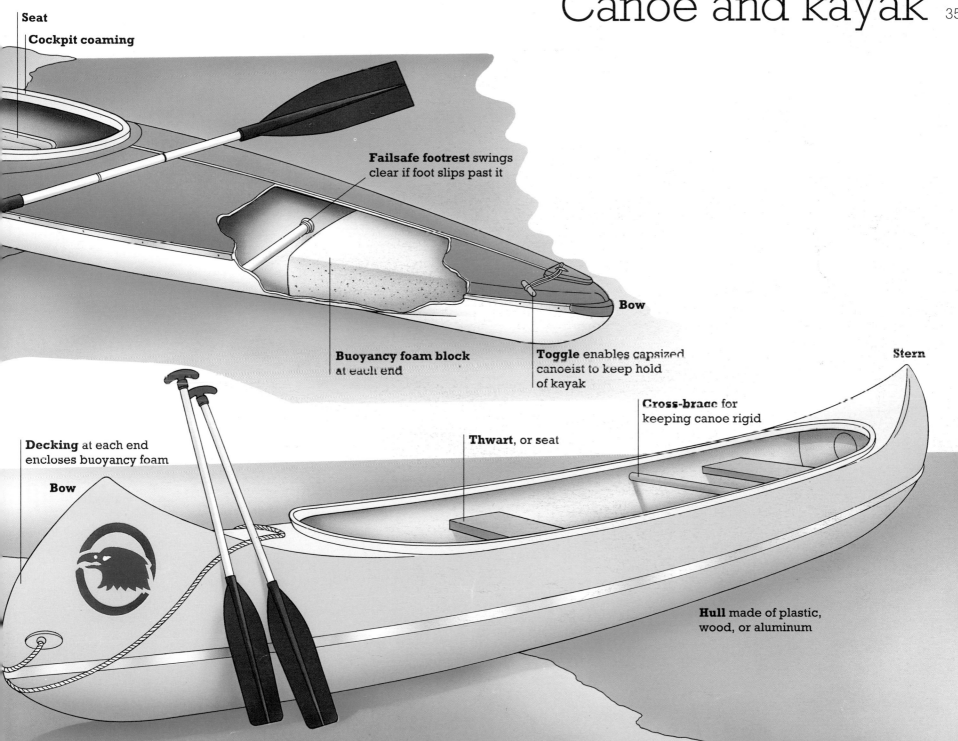

Seat

Cockpit coaming

Failsafe footrest swings
clear if foot slips past it

Bow

Buoyancy foam block
at each end

Toggle enables capsized
canoeist to keep hold
of kayak

Stern

Cross-brace for
keeping canoe rigid

Thwart, or seat

Decking at each end
encloses buoyancy foam

Bow

Hull made of plastic,
wood, or aluminum

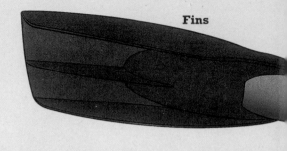

Fins

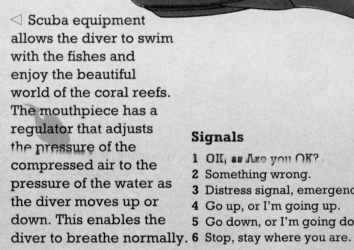

◁ Scuba equipment
allows the diver to swim
with the fishes and
enjoy the beautiful
world of the coral reefs.
The mouthpiece has a
regulator that adjusts
the pressure of the
compressed air to the
pressure of the water as
the diver moves up or
down. This enables the
diver to breathe normally.

Signals

1 OK, or Are you OK?
2 Something wrong.
3 Distress signal, emergency.
4 Go up, or I'm going up.
5 Go down, or I'm going down.
6 Stop, stay where you are.

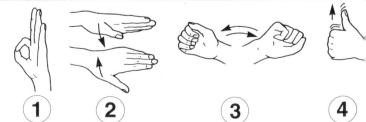

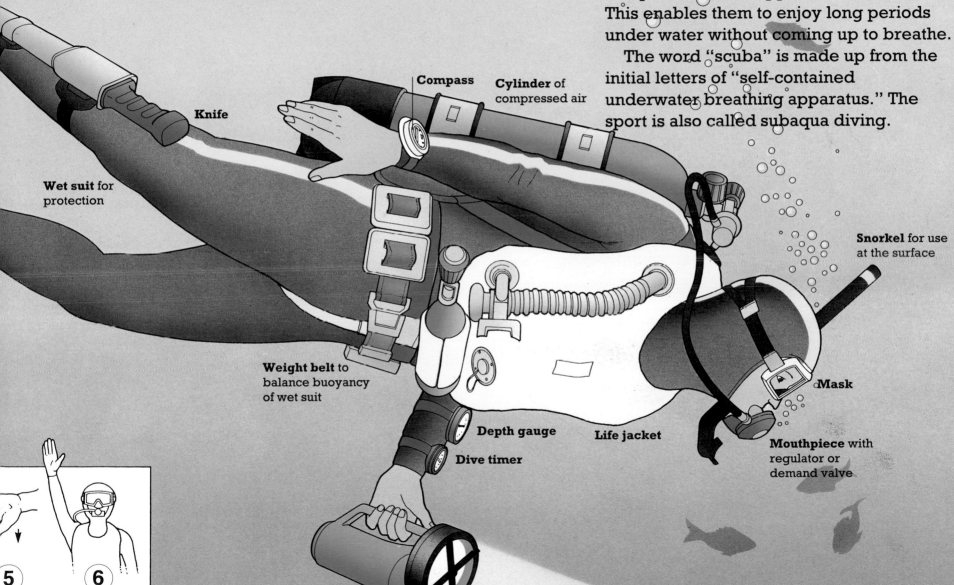

Scuba diver

Scuba divers have a cylinder of compressed air strapped to their back. This enables them to enjoy long periods under water without coming up to breathe.

The word "scuba" is made up from the initial letters of "self-contained underwater breathing apparatus." The sport is also called subaqua diving.

Knife

Compass

Cylinder of compressed air

Wet suit for protection

Snorkel for use at the surface

Weight belt to balance buoyancy of wet suit

Depth gauge

Dive timer

Life jacket

Mask

Mouthpiece with regulator or demand valve

5 **6**

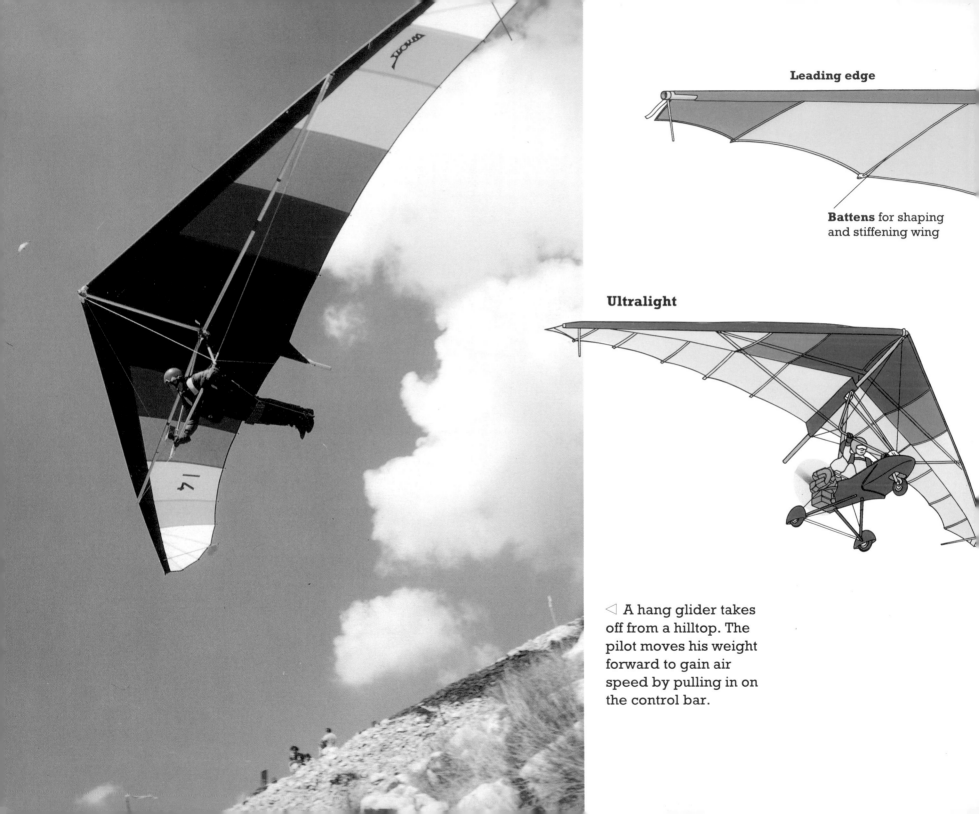

Leading edge

Battens for shaping
and stiffening wing

Ultralight

◁ A hang glider takes
off from a hilltop. The
pilot moves his weight
forward to gain air
speed by pulling in on
the control bar.

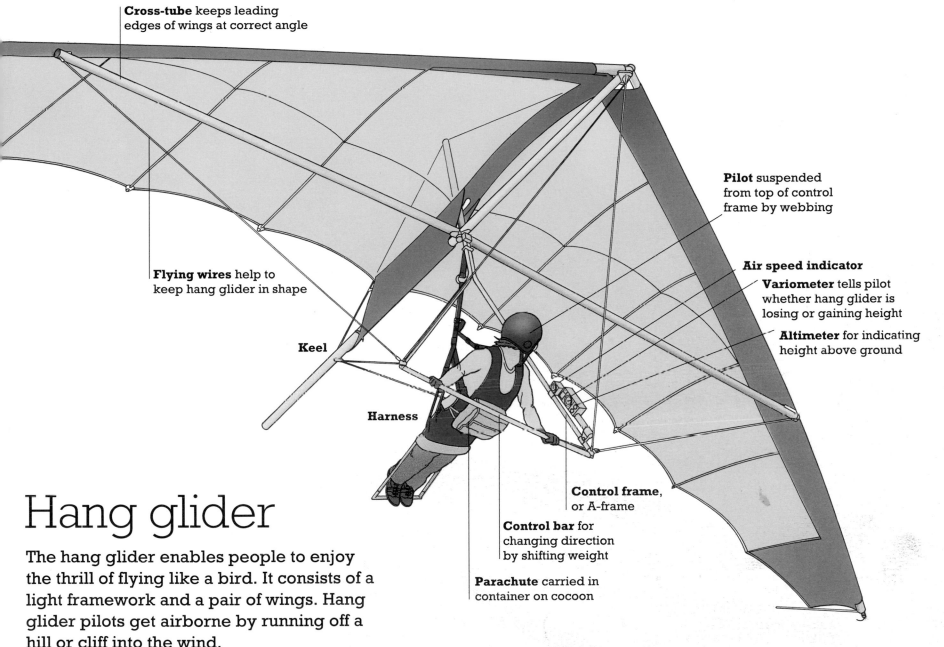

Cross-tube keeps leading edges of wings at correct angle

Flying wires help to keep hang glider in shape

Keel

Harness

Pilot suspended from top of control frame by webbing

Air speed indicator

Variometer tells pilot whether hang glider is losing or gaining height

Altimeter for indicating height above ground

Control frame, or A-frame

Control bar for changing direction by shifting weight

Parachute carried in container on cocoon

Hang glider

The hang glider enables people to enjoy the thrill of flying like a bird. It consists of a light framework and a pair of wings. Hang glider pilots get airborne by running off a hill or cliff into the wind.

There are also powered hang gliders. These machines, called ultralights, use small engines.

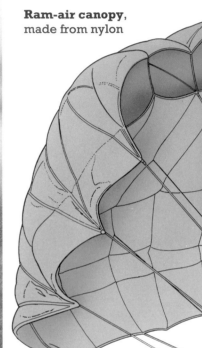

Ram-air canopy, made from nylon

Pilot chute, pulls main parachute from pack

◁ A team of parachutists link up in formation as they are falling. This is called relative work. Using chiefly their arms and legs, skydivers can vary their speed of fall by adopting different positions.

Skydiver

Skydiving is the popular name for sport parachuting. Parachutists jump out of aircraft and perform routines in the air before opening their parachutes.

The part of the jump before the parachute is opened is called freefall. Modern parachutes, called ram-air canopies, enable the parachutist to control his or her landing.

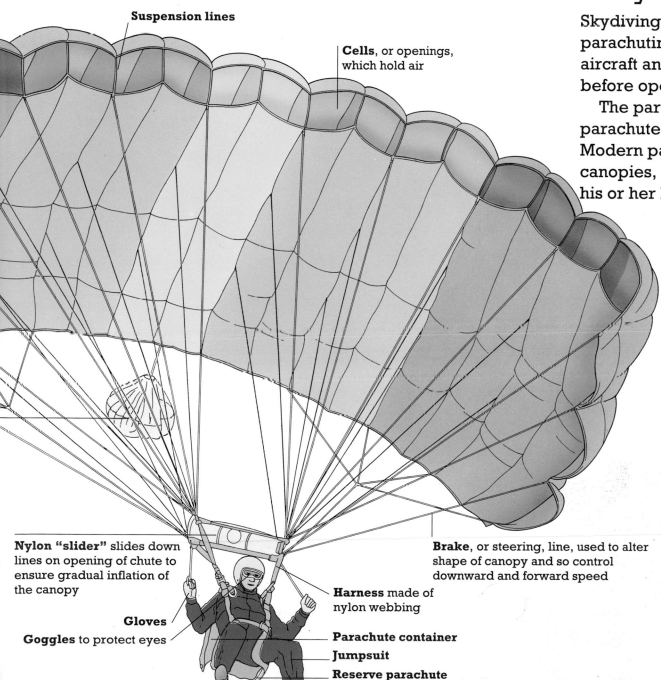

Suspension lines

Cells, or openings, which hold air

Nylon "slider" slides down lines on opening of chute to ensure gradual inflation of the canopy

Gloves

Goggles to protect eyes

Harness made of nylon webbing

Parachute container

Jumpsuit

Reserve parachute

Brake, or steering, line, used to alter shape of canopy and so control downward and forward speed

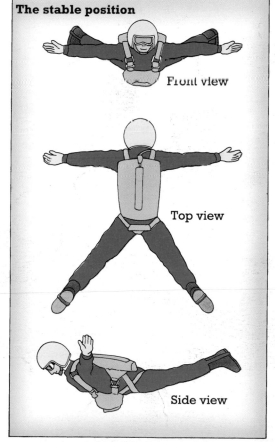

Freefall

The stable position

Front view

Top view

Side view

Ramp, or ski tower

1 Ski jumper adopts crouched stance called the "tuck" position for maximum speed on the chute, or in-run

◁ High above the ground, like a skydiver without a parachute, a ski jumper shows perfect style and control as he soars through the air.

1

2

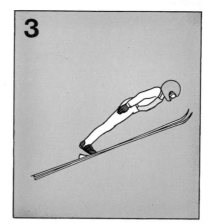

3

4

3 For the ideal position in flight, the body should be as straight as possible and almost parallel with the skis, arms held at sides – ski poles are not used in ski jumping

Judges' box

4 Landing must be clean, with knees and hips bent to absorb the impact and arms held out for balance. The skis should be close together, with one foot in front of the other. The hands must not touch the skis or the ground.

2 At takeoff, the jumper straightens his knees and stretches his body in a firm, powerful action

Out-run

Ski jump

Ski jumping is a daredevil sport and a thrilling spectacle to watch. Fearless competitors take off from huge ramps and soar gracefully through the air before landing as much as 330 feet (100 m) away.

Ski jumpers earn points for their style in the air and on landing as well as for distance jumped.

Firsts and records

The first grand prix

The first motor racing grand prix was staged at Le Mans, France, in 1906. The winning car was a Renault (shown left). It reached speeds of more than 62 mph (100 km/h). Its chassis (the frame to which engines, wheels, and bodywork are attached) was made of steel.

Turbocharged engine

A device called a turbocharger uses exhaust gases to boost engine power. The exhaust gases spin a turbine wheel. This is joined to a second turbine, called the impeller. This sucks in air, which is forced into the engine intake for more power.

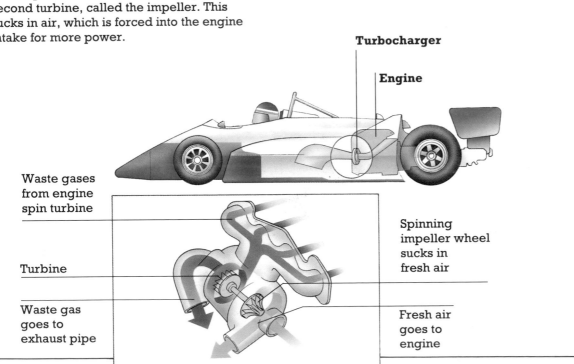

Turbocharger

Engine

Waste gases from engine spin turbine

Turbine

Waste gas goes to exhaust pipe

Spinning impeller wheel sucks in fresh air

Fresh air goes to engine

Drivers' helmets

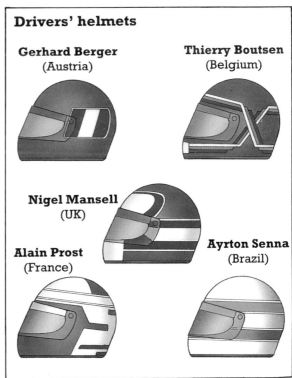

Gerhard Berger
(Austria)

Thierry Boutsen
(Belgium)

Nigel Mansell
(UK)

Alain Prost
(France)

Ayrton Senna
(Brazil)

△ The helmets of some leading Formula One drivers are shown above. They are as colorful and individual as their cars.

Mercedes – winner of the 1989 Le Mans

Le Mans endurance race

The 24-hour race for sports cars at Le Mans, in France, is the world's longest road race. Each car has two or three drivers, who take it in turns to drive while their partners rest. It is a tough test for both drivers and machines. The cars lap the circuit throughout the day and night at speeds reaching nearly 250 mph (400 km/h).

Land speed record

The holder of the world land speed record is said to be the fastest person on earth. To break the record, a vehicle must make two runs in opposite directions over either a mile or a kilometer. It's the average speed that counts. The car has a "flying start," reaching full speed before the starting mark.

Most land speed attempts take place on dry salt flats.

Pursuit racing

Pursuit racing is a cycling event in which riders start at opposite sides of the oval track. They try to catch each other in a set number of laps. If neither manages this by the end of the race, the winner is the one with the better time.

△ British driver Richard Noble, with *Thrust 2*, in which he set a land speed record in 1983 in Nevada.

△ *Thrust 2* jets across the Black Rock Desert to set a land speed record of 633 mph (1,019 km/h).

Pursuit bike

Speed on water

Speeds of over 340 mph (550 km/h) have been achieved in hydroplanes, motorboats that skim the surface of the water. The speed record for sailing vessels was set by a windsurfer, Pascal Maka of France, with 49 mph (79 km/h) in 1990.

△ Pascal Maka and his sailboard, the fastest non-powered craft on water.

Stunts and strange machines

◁ German rider Wilhelm Herz aboard his record-breaking NSU 500 speed bike.

Speed on two wheels

Wilhelm Herz went into the record books when he hit 180 mph (290 km/h) on an NSU 500 motorcycle in 1951. The run took place on a German autobahn (highway). Herz trained for his record attempt by baking bread! He kneaded dough to strengthen his forearms so that he could keep control of his bike at high speed.

BMX Stunts

The diagrams on the right show how to do some simple BMX stunts.

Rear-wheel pogo – 1 Standing behind the bike, put on the back brake and pull the front wheel off the ground. **2** Stand on level pedals, pull hard on the bars and lift the bike up and back. **3** Now heave the bike off the ground to pogo backward.

Bunny hop – 1 Ride toward the obstacle, keeping your weight over the middle of the bike. **2** As you near the obstacle, lift up the front wheel. **3** As soon as the wheel is over the obstacle, push forward and flick the back wheel up.

How to do a rear-wheel pogo.

① ② ③

How to do a bunny hop.

① ② ③

△ Stunts on two wheels are not uncommon – unless they happen to be on a six-wheel truck. The driver uses a ramp to set the vehicle on its side wheels. It then calls for a great deal of skill to drive it like this for a mile or more!

Electric power

Attempts to produce a satisfactory car running on electric power have so far proved unsuccessful. Yet in the early days of road travel, battery-powered cars were the fastest vehicles on the roads.

Many of the early record-breakers had motors powered by electricity supplied by batteries. Belgian driver Camille Jenatzy set a new land speed record in his bullet-shaped electric car *La Jamais Contente* ("Never Satisfied") in 1899. Known as the "Red Devil" because of his large red beard, he averaged 66 mph (106 km/h) over a flying kilometer. The record stood until 1902, when a steam car managed a speed of 75 mph (120 km/h). A replica of Jenatzy's car, built in 1989, was driven at 68 mph (109 km/h).

Jenatzy's car

△ An illustration of over a hundred years ago shows how people devised a way to control their movements on ice by maneuvering hand-held sails.

▷ A combination of sailboarding and skiing skills is needed to operate this "ski-sailor." A sailboarding rig is used and the mast is adapted to join the two skis.

▽ This long-distance tandem sailboard seems well equipped for a long journey. The "board" looks more like the hull of a boat and the sail rigs have a very unusual design.

Unusual sailing devices

People have used sailing boats for thousands of years. But it was a long time before the "personal rig" came into use. Skaters in the 1800s held a sail to make use of the wind. Sailboards became popular in the 1960s. They have now been adapted for use on snow.

Index